Old DROMORE, HILLSBOROUGH and DC

by

John Hanna, with photographs from the Des Quail collecti

Dromore Town Hall was built on the site of a market house which had been erected in 1732, and as it was situated within Market Square the new building was also used as a market house; it was one of the last of these to be built in Ireland. With the reorganisation of local government in the early 1970s it became redundant and the chamber is now used for local meetings. As can be seen there was once a cinema in the upstairs room which was run by a Robert Dale, and at the same time the building also provided accommodation for public meetings, entertainments, and the monthly Court of Petty Sessions. At one time prices for the cinema were one shilling for booked seats, and 2d. for the rest. The gates and railings were removed during the Second World War to make munitions, but have since been replaced.

First published in the United Kingdom, 2002,
by Stenlake Publishing,
Telephone / Fax: 01290 551122

ISBN 1 84033 198 4

FURTHER READING

The books listed below were used by the author during his research. None of them are available from Stenlake Publishing. Those interested in finding out more are advised to contact their local bookshop or reference library.

John Barry, *Hillsborough*, Universities Press (Belfast) Ltd, 1982.
May Blair, *Once Upon the Lagan*, The Blackstaff Press, 1981.
Andrew Doloughan, *Our Great Inheritance* Vols. 1, 2 and 3, Banbridge Chronicle Press, 1995.
E.R.R. Green, *The Lagan Valley 1800–1850*, Faber and Faber, 1949.
Grenfell Morton, *Railways in Ulster*, Friar's Bush Press, 1989.
Simon Walker, *Hillsborough – An Illustrated History and Companion*, Cottage Publications, 1994.

ACKNOWLEDGEMENTS

The author wishes to thank Cecil Allen and May Wethers of Donaghcloney, Victor McKinstry of Dromore, Harry Bell of Hillsborough, the staff of Dromore Public Library, and Miss McBride of the Scout Association.

The Dromore Drugstore – a title which perhaps would be more appropriate on the other side of the Atlantic. Dale's Pharmacy also had a city depot, presumably in Belfast. One of their specialities was 'Dale's Rheumatism and Sciatica Remedy – Proprietor and Originator, James Dale – Practical and Effective – Use It and Get Quick Relief – Excellent Testimonials.' The location of this building is uncertain; it certainly does not appear to be the same site as shown on page 9.

INTRODUCTION

DROMORE grew up on the site of a monastery which was established about AD 500 when the Abbey and See of Dromore were founded by Saint Colman. This probably accounts for the haphazard arrangement of the town's narrow hilly streets ('Dromore' is derived from the Gaelic *Druim Mor*, which means 'great ridge or back of a hill'). Its development was also helped by its position at the crossroads of the roads between Carrickfergus and Dublin, and Downpatrick and Armagh. The Vikings plundered the town in the ninth and tenth centuries and in 1177 Norman invaders built the fort which stood at the Mound. Cathedral status was granted in 1240.

In 1641 the town and cathedral were burnt by Irish rebels and it remained in ruins until 1661. In 1689 the first battle of the Williamite Campaign, the Break of Dromore, took place just outside the town. The names of some parts of the town – Cannon Hill, Gallows Street, Rampart Street – reflect this turbulent period.

By the end of the seventeenth century linen weaving had been introduced to the area by Huguenot immigrants. This industry developed throughout the following century and in the 1800s technological innovation led to further expansion. The first Market House was built in 1732 and by the early 1800s Dromore had the only flax market in the Lagan Valley. In the mid-nineteenth century the population was 2,110; by 1996 the figure was 3,400 and is still on the increase.

The earliest settlement in the HILLSBOROUGH area was Fox Fort, the home of the Magennes Clan who once controlled large areas of Co. Down. Later, the Normans built a fort (in addition to the one at Dromore) just to the north of where the village now stands. The area was initially known as Cromlyn and the earliest evidence of religious settlement is the twelfth century Chapel of Cromlyn.

In 1611 Sir Moyses Hill, an Englishman, bought local land from the Magennes family and it was Hill's son, Peter, who began the development of Hillsborough by building a fort on the Carrickfergus to Dublin Road. He also added a church and some dwellings. Like Dromore, the village and church were destroyed in the 1641 rebellion and it wasn't until the early 1660s that Colonel Arthur Hill began to repair the damage. He had remodelled the fort in 1650 and in 1662 built a new church. The village was also made a borough that year which allowed it to establish a town corporation and send two representatives to the Irish Parliament. Until these seats were abolished in 1800 one of the representatives was always a member of the Hill family.

Trevor Hill was made a baron and viscount in 1717. His son, Wills Hill, succeeded in 1742 and he developed Hillsborough into most of its present form. Hillsborough Castle was begun in 1758 and many of the present houses were built between 1750 and 1780. He also restored and rebuilt the church and built the Market House to encourage the linen trade.

By 1809 the Hills' Downshire Estate was one of the largest in Ireland, but by the end of the nineteenth century they were uprooting back to England. The castle was sold to the Northern Ireland Government in 1924 and, renamed Government House, it was home to Governors of Northern Ireland until 1973. It then reverted to its former name and has since been the residence of the Secretary of State for Northern Ireland.

DONAGHCLONEY means 'the church in the meadow' and the parish dates back six centuries. However, the history of the village is more closely tied to the development of the linen industry and in particular to the factory that was built there.

One of the pioneering families of the linen trade in Co. Down were the Nicholsons who had been connected to Donaghcloney since the late 1600s. When Thomas Nicholson purchased local land in 1796 he was described as a 'linen draper' which meant that he was a merchant who bought the cloth woven by the peasant weavers, financed the bleaching of it, and then sold it in the linen halls of the larger towns. Thomas's two sons, William and George, went on to expand this business and records of the Linen Board from 1816 show that they were two of the principal buyers in the Banbridge Linen Market. In 1813 another entrepreneur, John Shaw Brown, built the first part of the Donaghcloney factory which had a green capable of bleaching 10,000 pieces per year. In 1826 a £20 grant was given to all the weavers of Donaghcloney and Banoge so that they could start using improved damask looms.

By 1834 the Nicholsons had a bleach green and beetling mill at Banoge Bridge near Donaghcloney, and in 1836 the eldest son, William, purchased Banoge flour mill which he converted into a bleach works. In 1837 the second son, Robert, purchased the Brown's bleach green and other land so that by 1842 the two brothers owned practically the whole of the area of Donaghcloney and Banoge.

In 1866 Robert and William Nicholson were eventually succeeded by William Liddell (the two families had long been connected by marriage) and he bought the village two years later. Donaghcloney then became the centre for cambric weaving and handkerchief hemstitching, and throughout the world its damask linens graced the finest tables, including those of the *Titanic*.

The Liddell family remained in control until 1977 when they sold it to the Housing Association at the unbelievable sum of £163 per house as the buildings had become an expensive liability. In recent years the factory has had a number of owners; Bairds of Lurgan are the current managers, having taken over from Ewart Liddell (itself formed by a merger of the Ewart and Liddell firms).

The original Dromore Cathedral was burnt down in 1641 along with the rest of the town. It was rebuilt later in 1600s by the celebrated Bishop of the See, Jeremy Taylor. He is buried in the cathedral alongside his wife. The cathedral also houses a bible dating from 1613, a gift from John Straker who was a local gentleman. The stone cross was placed in its grounds in 1887, having originally stood in Market Square. It is thought to be over 1,000 years old. It was toppled when the Cromwellian Army defeated the Royalists at Dromore in September 1649, but was re-erected in the Square in 1654. The castle is believed to have been built in 1611 by William Worsley for the protection of his brother-in-law who was Bishop of Dromore. It has been a ruin for centuries, which is not surprising considering that in 1786 a local linen manufacturer removed a substantial part of its stone for building materials!

THE TOWN HALL AND OLD STOCKS, DROMORE. NO. 8.

Dromore Town Hall was built in 1886 and the clock tower was added four years later as a gift from William Cowan Heron of Maryfield, Holywood. This is recorded on the right hand plaque on the wall, but the other plaque has disappeared. The clock was supplied by Berringer Brothers, Belfast, and the bell was cast and hung by M. Byrne of Fountain Head Bell Foundry, Dublin. The clock face is 44 inches in diameter. The old stocks were much used for the punishment of petty offences and between 1805 and 1886 they stood at the south-west corner of Market Square. They were remounted in their present position on the base of the old Market Cross in front of the town hall in 1910.

The Wednesday fowl and pork market, which always attracted dozens of horse-drawn vehicles into Dromore's Market Square. The fowl always had their legs tied together and the pigs, which would have been slaughtered on the farm earlier, were covered with a white sheet in order to comply with the very basic hygiene regulations of the day. The last market of this kind was held in 1956 and the area shown is now called the Shambles, reflecting its previous use as a flesh market.

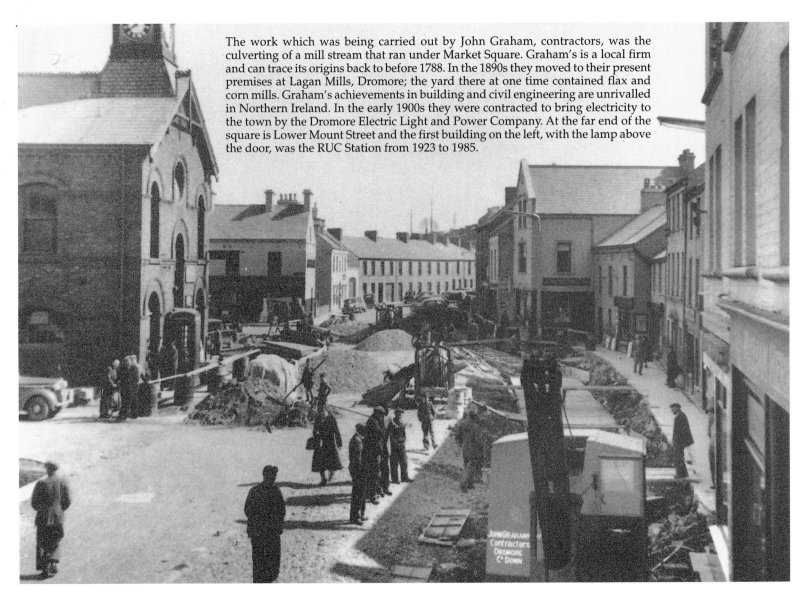

The work which was being carried out by John Graham, contractors, was the culverting of a mill stream that ran under Market Square. Graham's is a local firm and can trace its origins back to before 1788. In the 1890s they moved to their present premises at Lagan Mills, Dromore; the yard there at one time contained flax and corn mills. Graham's achievements in building and civil engineering are unrivalled in Northern Ireland. In the early 1900s they were contracted to bring electricity to the town by the Dromore Electric Light and Power Company. At the far end of the square is Lower Mount Street and the first building on the left, with the lamp above the door, was the RUC Station from 1923 to 1985.

Seen on a market day sometime before the war memorial was erected, the quality of the buildings surrounding the square is obvious. Dromore had numerous hotels including the Central Hotel and Napier's Hotel which occupy the two premises to the right. These two buildings have been restored as a public house and off-license owned by Mulholland's. The building to the left of Josiah Ward, Direct Importer and Wine Merchant, has been demolished, but the one on his right has housed Dromore Post Office since 1982.

The war memorial remembers those 'who made the supreme sacrifice for King and Empire' in both world wars. For the First World War there are over one hundred names listed, while the losses numbered seventeen for the 1939–45 conflict. Princes Street, which leads to Hillsborough Road, is named after the Prince Regent, later King George IV, who visited Dromore in place of his father, King George III, who was incapacitated. While in the town he called to see the Rev. James Bankhead who was the minister of First Presbyterian (Non-subscribing) Church in Rampart Street. The large building on the right is now derelict, while the smaller building with the arched doorway is the premises of M.A. Quail, butcher.

On the south-west corner of Market Square at the start of Church Street is the fine building designed by the local architect Henry Hobart. It became one of the premises of Dale's Pharmacy. On the opposite corner were the premises of McMurray Brothers who were drapers, outfitters, and boot and shoe merchants. This latter building is currently occupied by P.E. Neeson's electrical goods store, while the pharmacy is currently unoccupied. Another fine building to the left with the pitched roof was once the Excel Boot and Shoe Store.

Church Street was part of the main Belfast to Dublin road before the introduction of the bypass. The first building on the left has remained a branch of the Northern Bank since the time of this photograph, while the building with the high roof halfway down on the right hand side was rebuilt as a branch of the Ulster Bank in 1910. The third building on the right is still Small and Company, a general drapery store. This family firm has traded from this site for over 150 years. On the other side of the street the building with the lamp above the door was the Stag's Head bar. The first building on the right is Dromore Post Office, which was run by Mrs Mary McCleery, before being transferred to Market Square.

Church Street, looking past the cathedral towards Market Square. All the houses on the left opposite the cathedral were demolished in the early 1970s and replaced by a housing development. The gates to the rectory may be seen at the junction with Regent Street, and behind the trees the two buildings still remain.

Meeting St., Dromore.

Many of the houses in Meeting Street were modest two storey houses built for the textile workers in the 1870s. The building with the ornate porch was the Crown Hotel, later known just as the Crown. It was owned by the Patterson family. In recent years the building became the Brewery Inn, but it is now empty and has been allowed to deteriorate. Right at the end of the street on the left hand side, beyond the junction, are the two houses which were taken down and rebuilt brick by brick in the Ulster Folk and Transport Museum so that their period interiors could become historical exhibits.

Meeting Street, looking towards Bridge Street. The first building on the left was used as the Orange Hall during the Second World War, when the actual hall was used as a billet for the Army. Further up the street, on the right, the building with the three dormer windows had a shop in which the wife of the famous inventor Harry Ferguson, designer of the Ferguson tractor, once worked. The Woollen Hall, the large shop in the centre of the picture, was demolished in the 1980s to make way for an extension of Meeting Street to ease the traffic in Market Square.

Prince's Street leads north out of the town towards Hillsborough and was once part of the main road to Belfast. The buildings shown have not changed much. The house with dormer windows on the right was once an RUC station; there is still evidence of the cells in its basement. On the left, the building next to the one with the wrought iron railings is Rath House, built in 1780 and one of the oldest buildings in Dromore. Appropriately, it now houses an antique shop.

Bridge Street, looking towards Market Square and the bridge over the Lagan. This view has changed little over the years. Mrs Jardine's bar and spirit store is now the Bridge Bar. The first shop on the right was Castle's who specialised in 'youth's and boy's suits'.

A view from Bridge Street, taken just across the bridge and looking up to the junction of Meeting Street and Rampart Street. Most of these buildings are still in place. The large shop on the corner beyond the junction is now Robert Bogg's butcher's shop. Barr's was a milliners and outfitters, but was demolished in the 1980s to make room for the Elim Pentecostal Church. The premises just in view on the left was a draper's shop, while the tall building beyond it on the same side was a boot and shoe shop; both of these were owned by the Castle brothers.

Gallows Street leads out of the north-west corner of Market Square. Few of the buildings on the left such as the nearest one (which was the Masonic Hall) remain, while all those on the right are still standing. The second building on the right was once owned by Dan Sloan, a draper, while a Thompson's of Perth sign indicates an agent who sold dyes. This photograph was used as a postcard and local readers will notice that St Colman's Church appears to have been drawn in. It is not a true image and is too close to the road. A rose bed now marks the position, not shown in this picture, where the gallows used to be.

Regent Street is believed to be named after the Prince Regent, as is the Regent Bridge in the foreground. It was built in 1850 as a result of the upgrading of turnpike roads to take stage coaches. It replaced the Downshire Bridge, which was built in 1740 and was some 40 yards upstream. Regent Bridge was built from a combination of whinstone and granite from the nearby Mountains of Mourne. It has three semicircular arches with a total span of 75 feet. It says a lot for its construction that after forming a part of the main Belfast to Dublin road for over 150 years it still has no weight restrictions. One of the many town water pumps may be seen at the side of the road. The white building seen in the background at Church Street is the Rectory. The buildings on the right were demolished to make way for the extension of Meeting Street and a police station has been built where the railings are.

The 'go-as-you-please' race was actually a marathon from Belfast to Lurgan. The distance was twenty-six miles and several hundred yards and the journey had to be completed 'without extraneous assistance from vehicles'. On 22 June 1907 the streets of Dromore were bedecked with flags and large crowds thronged Market Square to cheer on the 461 participants who had been started at the Markets in Belfast by the High Sheriff of the city, Dr. P.R. O'Connell, at 1 p.m. According to a newspaper report, 'the streets of Lisburn, Hillsborough, Dromore and Waringstown were crowded to give the men their hearty plaudits'. Contrary to expectations the first arrivals in Lurgan took just over three hours, the first three being F.W. Furlonger, Thomas McCullough, and a Corporal Sparks. One hundred and sixty competitors finished before 6 p.m. and qualified for prizes. The promoter of the 1907 event was the *Ireland Saturday Night* sports paper and they tried to revive it in the 1950s, without much success.

This comfortable square Georgian house was built by Bishop Beresford in 1781, and was the See House. The following year it became the home of Bishop Thomas Percy until his death in 1811. He laid out the grounds. It continued to be occupied by the Bishops of Dromore until the end of 1842. It was then sold to Mr James Quinn JP, who lived there until his death in 1883. A community of Jesuit Fathers purchased it, using it from 1884 to 1888, and renamed it Loyola House. They retained possession until 1918 when it passed to Captain Thomas Herbert Wallace MC, JP, LLB. Later, it lay vacant for some time before being demolished. The Dromore Golf Club had a nine-hole course in the grounds from 1895 to 1910, when the club ceased to exist.

The Second Presbyterian Church on Banbridge Road is little changed today. Its history can be traced as far back as 1836 when the local Presbyterians approached the Synod for a church. The building started in 1841 and the first minister was ordained in 1843. Since 1908 it has been known as Banbridge Road Presbyterian Church and a church hall was built alongside it in 1961. The inset pictures shows the Rev. James Rentoul, formerly of Clough in Co. Antrim. He was appointed as minister in May 1878 and remained in the position until his death on 2 June 1917.

The Cottage Hospital was built and endowed by William Cowan Heron in 1898 as a gift to the people of Dromore. When it closed in 1994 there was considerable protest, but all to no avail. It was said that it was a pity those responsible had not abided by the Biblical quotation above the front door which read 'Comfort ye my people, saith the Lord'. Used as a geriatric unit since 1974, the building has now been redeveloped as sheltered housing. The architect of the building was Henry Hobart, who designed many of the prominent buildings in Dromore, including the Ulster Bank in Church Street. William Cowan Heron, who died aged ninety-seven in 1917, also left money for the annual maintenance of the building.

Following the 1641 rebellion parcels of land were handed out to officers in lieu of pay in the hope that they would settle in Ulster. A captain in the Troop of Horse, John Magill (who was later knighted), acquired several parcels and at Dromore he built this mansion which later became known as Gill Hall. A descendant of Magill was Lord Clanwilliam. The house was built in the early 1670s and is reputed to have been one of Ireland's most haunted houses. When the fifth Earl of Clanwilliam brought his bride to Gill Hall in 1909, apparently she found the ghostly residents too much to bear and they made a hasty retreat for their home at Montalto, near Ballynahinch. They never returned to the house, although it was later home for part of the year to a Mr Augustus Brush. It was badly damaged by a fire in May 1970 and the dangerous remains were demolished by Territorial Army experts.

The Mound is one of the finest examples of a Norman motte and bailey castle in Ireland. It is 60 feet high and has a circumference of 600 feet. At one time the bailey, or lower courtyard, would have been protected by timber palisading, while an archery tower would have been positioned on the mound to give a good all-round view of the River Lagan and the surrounding countryside. It is thought William de Coercy built the castle shortly after the Norman Conquest, although some historians believe that it could be even older. The buildings in the foreground are the Lagan Mills site of John Graham, contractors.

While most of the linen industry in Dromore was based around hemstitching, in 1910 Messrs Murphy and Stevenson built this large weaving factory, which had five hundred looms, in an area known as the Holm. This is outside the town on the Lurgan Road and in this photograph is viewed from the south bank of the River Lagan. The firm also built a number of dwelling houses for the workers and these can be seen to the left of the chimney. On the right is the workers' football field. The factory was taken over by the firm of Ewart Liddell and they subsequently transferred to Donaghcloney. While the chimney has gone, the factory buildings are now occupied by Mulgrew Transport and the housing still remains.

The viaduct at Dromore has seven arches and crosses the River Lagan at what is now the town park. It was designed by Thomas Jackson for the Banbridge, Lisburn and Belfast Railway which was later absorbed by the Great Northern Railway (Ireland). It enabled the railway to reach Banbridge, which it did in 1863. It was further extended to Newcastle and locals could take an excursion to the seaside town for 1/3d. or a return fare to Belfast on a Saturday for two shillings. When the railway closed in 1956 there was a danger that this fine construction would be demolished. Fortunately, the local council was able to purchase it for the grand sum of £15. In the background may be seen the chimney of the Holm Factory further down the river.

Gilwell Park in England was opened as a Scout Officer's Training Centre in 1919. General A.R. Ricardo, Commissioner for Ulster, wished to have a similar instruction camp in Ireland and early in 1923 Lord Clanwilliam offered the free use of Gill Hall. The site was considered ideal and among efforts to provide funds for the training courses were the production of two plays in the Hippodrome Theatre, Belfast, and a 'Grand Indoor Rally' in the Ulster Hall, Belfast, in March 1923. Several courses were held in the first year and the men pictured here were the officers from throughout Northern Ireland who took the second one, held between 25 May and 3 June. In 1939 the 'Scouter's Training Camp' moved to Antrim Castle. *Back row* (from left to right): J.K. Beattie, T. Stringer, W. Smyth, W. Gough, H.W. Bryson, S. McDonald, J.C. Eaton; *middle row*: S.D. Irons, E. Brownell, R.T. Clarke, B. Fielding Smith, W. Dunne, A. Sterrett, F.H. Fullerton, R.C. MacDonnell; *front row*: H.E. Keown, C.H. Meagher, Rev. R.H. Wheelan, F.J. Hunter, Lt. Col. G. Drage DSO, W.J. Watts.

The lower end of Hillsborough's Main Street at the junction between Lisburn Street, to the left, and Ballynahinch Street. The statue – the work of Samuel Ferres Lynn and erected in 1868 – is of Arthur, fourth Marquis of Downshire. He was born on 6 August 1812 and died on 6 August 1868. Just here there is a small park. As early as 1810 this was the site of a brewery, which was built in the gothic style in keeping with the church opposite. In front of the park is a garden commemorating Arthur Stanley Boyd MD, FRCCP, who died in 1971. He was the fourth generation of the Boyd family to serve as a doctor in Hillsborough. The advertisement for the famous Ulster cigarette 'Gallaher's Blues' is on the wall of the shop which is still owned by the Thompson family after nearly eighty years. In the centre of the picture M. Clarke's shop, a ladies outfitter, is now a branch of the Ulster Bank. The large building in the background is the Downshire School which later became a church hall when a new primary school was built further up Ballynahinch Street.

Main Street, Hillsborough. The small building to the left was originally one of two school buildings which were connected to the parish church and is on the right hand side of the avenue leading to the church. This one was the boy's school and is now a church hall. The Celtic cross is the memorial to the dead of the two world wars, when many young men from the village volunteered to serve, including Arthur, seventh Marquis of Downshire. The memorial was erected around 1921 and paid for by public subscription.

A short Main Street leads steeply uphill from the parish church to the Market House and the castle. In fact it was once called Castle Street. On the left the stone-dressed building was probably built in the seventeenth century. When this picture was taken they contained shop premises, but in the early 1980s it was refurbished to become private dwellings, although the window structure remains the same. The next building down remains the butcher's shop of J. Walker. The white building next door, No. 21, is 'Hillside' which has been a public house since 1777. The shop on the right with the bicycle outside is now the gift shop, Cowdy Crafts.

Dating from the 1930s this view from the top of Main Street shows on the right the gates to the Fort. All the buildings on either side of the gates remain intact; the building on the immediate right was once the premises of John Hunter, spirit dealer. To the left of the gates is The Plough, a well-known hostelry. At one time the road to Moira went in between the Market House on the left and the large Georgian terrace beyond. These houses were built in 1780 for the more affluent townsfolk. Lord Arthur Hill named the larger houses in the terrace after some of his Downshire ancestors, and these are Hill House, Blundell House, and Trevor House.

Around 1760 Wills Hill built the central block of the Market House to attract linen manufacturers to the town. In 1810 the north and south wings were added. The north wing was used as a courtroom until 1986. The courtroom has been restored and is open to the public. The central block now houses a tourist information office. The building has a square clock tower with ornamental urns, cupola, and banner weathervane.

Lisburn Street is the oldest part of town and most of its buildings remain, although the three storey house at the top in this picture has been demolished. The vacant space now provides access to a car park. Set back from the road between the two taller buildings on the left was the Masonic Hall and the building to its right was at one time Magill's grocery shop. There are a number of arched entries off to the right, one of which had the peculiar name of 'Squeezegut Entry'.

Around 1820 Lisburn Street was called Great Newport Street as at that time the local people had high hopes that the trade from the quay at Newport on the Lagan Navigation Canal would bring great prosperity to the region. The barges mainly carried coal for the local gasworks. This intersection was probably the site of the earliest buildings in the village. Evidence would suggest that the buildings on the left were once single storey cottages. Abraham Murray at one time owned the hairdressing establishment. He was also an excellent fiddler. The large building next door was a grocery shop owned by G. and H. Bell since the late 1860s, but is now a Mace store. The Bell family still has a number of businesses in the village including the Village Tea Room, which is now built into the old entry to the right of the hairdresser's sign.

Ballynahinch Street was once called New Street. The building on the left is Downshire Hall. This was originally the Downshire School which opened in 1887 and served in this function until 1958 when it became the church hall. On the right hand side, just past the entrance to Arthur Street, is the house where the composer and conductor Sir Hamilton Harty lived from shortly after his birth in 1880 until his death in 1941. At the head of Arthur Street is a listed building which was the blacksmith's forge. On the left hand side the circular building is what remains of a coaching house. Further up the street the building with the Doric portico was formerly Blessington House. The first Marquis of Downshire built it as a residence for his agent. Part of the building has been a branch of the Northern Bank for a number of years. Just past this and behind the white wall was Law's yard and the entrance to a farmhouse. A new housing development, Hamilton Harty Court, was built on this site in 1992.

The old castle, known locally as the Fort so as not to be confused with Hillsborough Castle, was built on the site of the old Magennes stronghold and completed by Colonel Arthur Hill in 1650. It was constituted a Royal Fort by Letters Patent of King Charles II, which made Colonel Arthur the 'Hereditary Constable of Hillsborough Fort' with command of twenty warders. In 1690 King William III spent four nights at the Fort on his way south to the Battle of the Boyne. In 1758 Wills Hill remodelled the tower house into the gothic style building of today. It was handed over by the Hill family to the people of Northern Ireland in 1959.

The twenty 'wardours' granted to Colonel Hill by King Charles II were paid at the rate of sixpence a day. The warders were maintained at the Fort for nearly 300 years, although their uniforms changed from the buff jacket of the Stuart days to the gaily-barred tunics, buckskin breeches and cocked hats which the British troops who fought under King George II at Dettingen had worn. The sergeant, front row on the left, had a more impressive hat than the others and a red sash, while the bugler next to him wore the only uniform with epaulettes. Up until the latter part of last century the 'castlemen', as they were sometimes called, were a colourful sight on state occasions or as constables at the nearby Maze Races. The last survivor of the warders was William John Green who died in 1954 aged eighty-nine, and it is likely that he is in this photograph. Until the end of the 1990s a bugler was retained; this was Gerald Silcock who succeeded his uncle, Gerald Atkinson, who had himself succeeded his father, William George Atkinson, who was bugler in 1908, around the time of this photograph. One of these uniforms is on display in the Marquis of Downshire Tavern in Lisburn Street.

Hillsborough Church in Back ground.

Downshire Football Team 1910

Originally named the Downshire Young Mens' Football Club, Downshire F.C. continue to play in a strip of vertical red and white stripes. This is the team of 1910. In the early days of the club they played friendlies anywhere they could get opposition and travelled to away games in a horse and cart. Home games were played on the notorious sloping pitch at Dunbeg Park which was leased from the Marquis of Downshire at a cost of one shilling per year. The club moved to a new pitch with their own rooms at Old Coach Road on the outskirts of Hillsborough in 1992.

The Lagan Navigation Canal was opened in 1794 and along its length were a number of quays. One of these was at Newport and grain and coal for the distillery at Hillsborough was unloaded there. Throughout the nineteenth century and the early part of the twentieth the canal was a great asset to both agriculture and industry in the area. This view is of the viaduct, about a mile from the village, where the Banbridge, Lisburn & Belfast Railway line crossed the canal. The towpath for the horses which pulled the barges is on the left. It was the coming of the railways in 1863 that began to take the trade from the canal barges, although the canal remained open until 1954. The railway was also eventually closed and there is very little evidence of either mode of transport left today.

The north end of Donaghcloney. The village post office is on the left, while next door to the left the building with the ornate doorway was the Plough public house. It is said that it was never fully licensed and patrons had to stand as there were no chairs. The large building beyond the row on the left is the Orange Hall which was built in 1880 and is still in use today. The older building to the right was demolished, while the same fate was suffered by the post office and the public house in 1981 to make way for a grocery store and a filling station.

This view of the main street was taken prior to 1910, before the construction of Liddell Terrace. These cottages were built by the owners of the factory at that time, John Shaw Brown and Company.

It was common for the owners of factories at the start of the last century to build houses for their mill workers. Liddell Terrace is named after the owner of the mill, William Liddell. These houses were built around 1910, and the shop at the far end of the terrace was owned by Sam McDowell. He sold general hardware and was also a coal merchant. It later became the Co-op and is now the Donaghcloney Housing Association. The terrace beyond the shop was built earlier by John Shaw Brown and Company. The taller building contained a water tank which enabled the houses to have running water before many others in the area. All of this is still standing today.

A view of the main street from a position in front of the National School. Apart from the large house at the end of the street, all of the other buildings remain intact. Set into the larger house on the left is a datestone from 1742. The other houses on this side are Quality Row and Red Row. These parlour houses were built to high specifications for the mill workers, thus the name Quality Row. There is a link with Dromore as it was the builders John Graham who rebuilt Donaghcloney and the houses in the picture in the 1890s and early 1900s. The houses on the right are Liddell Terrace.

The Loyal Orange Institution was formed in September 1795 and held its first Battle of the Boyne Commemoration Parade on 12 July 1796. For the annual celebrations arches are erected for the parades to pass under, such as this one in Donaghcloney pictured in 1911. The arches contain various cultural and political symbols to indicate loyalty to the British monarch; this one also features biblical symbols such as Jacob's ladder and doves of peace.

In earlier, more paternalistic times, mill owners could play a large part in the social welfare of the villages where their workers lived. The tablet above this building reads 'Memorial School 1903 erected by the widow and children of William N. Liddell Esq. JP, Donacloney, to commemorate his useful life'. The buildings in the background are called Lagan Terrace and were the first mill houses to be built in the village towards the end of the nineteenth century. At one time they were called 'Ladysmith' to commemorate the relief of Ladysmith in 1900 during the Boer War. They are still there and have been extended to the left. The National School, as it was known, was closed in the late 1970s and became St Patrick's Church of Donaghcloney Parish. It was dedicated by the Right Reverend Dr R.H. Eames, the Bishop of Down and Dromore, in September 1980.

This view of the Donaghcloney factory is taken from the north side of the River Lagan, close to the local cricket ground. The drying sheds in the foreground are no longer in place, but the building behind the trees on the left was until recently the factory shop. Drying sheds, or 'lofts' as they were known, were heated with steam and used for conditioning yarn before bundling. In 1911 William Liddell employed 1,000 workers, but only 150 of them lived in the village. The Liddells were model employers and provided many recreational activities for their workers. William Liddell's sons introduced cricket to their workers here and the Donaghcloney club is one of a number of cricket clubs in Ulster associated with major linen manufacturers. It was formed in 1891, and the pavilion, which is still in use, was built in 1901. There was a cycling track around the cricket ground and the workers were also provided with an open-air swimming pool, tennis courts and allotments.

DONACLONEY FACTORY LOOKING SOUTH

As one looks at this view of the factory from across the dam today, it is hard to believe that so little has changed after so many years. Even the pipe and small weir remain, as do all the buildings and the chimney. The saw-edge sloping roofs to the left were the dressing shops and the winding department. The tall building with the little cupola on top was the engine room, which housed a steam engine. The three storey building next to the chimney, which now is the main office, was at one time the design centre. The date set into the porch above the door is 1898.

Rifle Range Construction, Donacloney. 1914.

Built and used by the Ulster Volunteer Force, the construction of this rifle range indicates clearly the difference between 1914 and our more advanced age. Each of the sandbags had to be carried in by hand and the hole was probably dug only with spades. This range was in the grounds of Banogue House, the family seat of the Liddells at Donaghcloney.